STORIES MY DAD TOLD ME

Tracilyn George

©2017 Tracilyn George

INTRODUCTION

My father came from a family of talkers and storytellers. Some family members exaggerated the details of their stories while others would make things up altogether.

Dad always wanted to put his stories in writing but, he was far too embarrassed by his spelling to do so. While his math skills were at genius level, his spelling left much to be desired.

Because of his poor spelling, mine was excellent. He often would ask me how to spell words from as far back as I could remember.

There were mumblings my father had put his tales in writing but, the papers were never found. Chances are they were inadvertently thrown out during a clean up of our attic.

Since his death in 2007, I had a lingering thought in the back of my head to write the tales he told me over the years. Most of the following stories are anecdotes from my father or about my father. There are also contributions from friends and family members.

WHEN YOU CROSS A SCOTTISH MUM

My father's mother came to Canada from Carluke, Scotland when she was 16 years old, hoping to become a teacher. She spoke only Gaelic and knew no one here. She never become a school teacher but taught her children right from wrong without putting her hands on them.

Dad said when he was younger, the summers in Dartmouth were hot and the water from the well was so cold, it would give you a headache.

One summer day, when my Dad was about twelve, his mother was on her knees, scrubbing the hardwood floors in the kitchen. He walked through the back door, dragging in dirt onto the floors she was on her knees, cleaning.

Nanny had scolded him. He gave her a saucy response and sat down at the kitchen table.

She didn't say a word. Nanny stood, took her bucket and dumped the dirty water into the sink. She then pumped fresh water into her bucket.

When she finished, she turned and threw the freezing cold water over my father's head. Dad sat in shock.

Nanny pointed her finger, stating, "That's for saucing me once. You do it again; you will get worse."

My father said he never gave her lip for the rest of his life.

BE CAREFUL HOW YOU ASK FOR SOMEONE

My father's first job was as a milkman. He worked with his brother, Harry, for the Woodlawn Dairy.

He often delivered to Conrad's Store on Albro Lake Road where my mother worked. One day, someone asked him to go to Conrad's and ask for her.

When he went in, he asked, "Who's Dollie Craig?"

Her response was, "I am. What's it to ya?"

Dad wasn't expecting her to be so abrupt and he was taken by surprise. He said when they married; he should have knocked her out. I told him if he had, they would hold his funeral that evening because Mum would have killed him.

SNOW BATHING

My dad always loved to talk. He never cared with who as long as he was having a conversation.

On one particular occasion, he was talking with a young black woman who frequently attended the bingo hall he managed. I don't know how they came about their conversation but, they were talking about sunbathing.

The young woman said, "I think white people want to be us. It's why they out in the sun. They want to be brown like me.

"You don't see black people laying out on the snow, trying to get white, do you?"

My father, who also enjoys a good argument, couldn't find a reason to do so. "I never thought of that," he conceded.

WHEN LITTLE PEOPLE ARE LISTENING

When my niece, Hanna, was younger, she spent a lot of time staying with my parents. She made things interesting at the house when she did. She always seemed to enjoy spending a few days with Nanny and Granddad George.

One night when she was about four – I was living in the Arctic at the time – she was visiting with them again. Hanna was playing with her toys while Mum and Dad were watching television.

My mother asked Dad to do something for her. Dad answered that he'll do it once the next commercial came on.

Hanna turned and piped up, "Granddad, you do as you're told. You know Nanny's the boss in this house."

Dad said she was serious in her scolding and it took a lot for him to keep from laughing. Neither he nor Mum thought she was even paying attention to them so it came to a shock to them when she gave them her two cents worth.

WHEN YOU DATE A FATHER'S GIRL

As I had stated earlier, my father met my mother at Conrad's Store. When they first started going out, they would attend to dances in North End Dartmouth every Friday night with a large group of friends.

Since my mother lived the closest to where the dances took place, the gang all went there after they were over. They planned their departure to catch the last trolley to go home. My mother lived on Albro Lake Road and my Dad lived on Joffre Street.

The two streets are quite a distance apart – about an hour's walk from each other. During the summer, it's not a bad walk but during the dead of winter, it could be brutal. So, catching the last trolley to the other side of the city in winter would be a good thing.

One Friday night after the dance, the group – about a dozen – went to Mum's place to warm up and sing songs before going to their homes. They left their mittens, scarves, coats and boots in the hallway and on the staircase.

About ten minutes after they arrived, my grandfather Craig came downstairs. He didn't say much; just watched and listened from the hallway.

When the group was ready to leave for the night, they found all of their belongings tied in knots. By the time they had everything untangled, they missed the last bus and had to walk home in the freezing cold.

The following week, they thought they would be smart and put everything in the dining room. Again, when they were ready to leave, they were all in knots; and again, they had to walk home.

Dad said he never saw my grandfather doing it and couldn't figure out how he did it with no one seeing him.

WHEN YOUR SON MAKES A FAMILY DECISION

In 1970, my parents decided they wanted to become foster parents. When my middle brother, John, found out the first foster child was coming; he skipped school to be there. My theory is he wanted to rub it in to my other brothers he was the first one to see her.

When the social worker came to drop the baby off, my Dad said the baby was head to toe in fecal matter. Mum handed the baby to Johnnie and instructed him to strip her while she ran a bath. She ordered him to throw the clothes in the fireplace once he finished.

Mum had brought down my brothers' old baby clothes to put on her until she could buy her new ones. The social worker, feeling sorry for the baby, also purchased her a stuffed teddy bear.

A couple months later, the social worker came back to take the foster child to another family. John was home when she arrived.

"You're not taking my sister," he stated, determined. Considering he was 6 feet and 250 pounds, few people would disagree with him even though he was a gentle giant.

The social worker wasn't sure what to say. Mum and Dad could have said no but felt obligated since Johnnie was not changing his mind. Until he passed away, I often teased my brother about his choosing me to be a part of the family and being the first to accept me.

CHOCOLATE MILK VS WHITE MILK

As mentioned, I was the first foster child my parents had. Over the years, they lost count of how many children they took in.

One child in particular, I still consider my brother over forty years later. He was in our care for over five years. My parents wanted to adopt him but his mother wouldn't sign the papers.

Tony is biracial and my family and I are Caucasian. Dad told me about one incident when we went grocery shopping with my mother.

Mum was pushing the cart and Dad walked behind her, carrying Tony in one arm and me in the other. Two older women kept giving us strange looks whenever they met us in the aisle.

Dad thought, 'I've had enough of this.' In the next aisle, he announced, "This happens when you feed one white milk and the other one chocolate." The two women couldn't get away fast enough.

DECEMBER 6, 1917

Not all of Dad's stories had a humorous side to them. Here is one that was more serious.

On December 6, 1917, a maritime disaster occurred in Halifax, NS. The SS Mont-Blanc, a cargo ship from France was carrying a load of high explosives. It collided with the Norwegian vessel SS Imo in the middle of Halifax Harbour.

A fire set ablaze the French ship's cargo on board. This caused a large explosion that devastated Halifax.

Nearly 2,000 people had been killed by blast, debris, fires and collapsed buildings, and it injured an estimated 9,000 others.

My grandmother Craig (my mother's mother) was working in the kitchen while my Uncle Joe – who was about 1 at the time – was taking a nap upstairs. She was at the sink when she saw sailors run past the window.

Instinct told her something was amiss. She went to Joe's bedroom and took him from his crib.

No sooner than she sat him at the table and turned to finish her dishes, there was a loud explosion. The kitchen window blew in. Shards of glass missed Uncle Joe by inches.

My grandmother cleaned up the mess before she headed back upstairs. The ceiling above my uncle's crib had fallen into where he had been sleeping.

GOD DOESN'T CARE

When I was growing up, I never knew my father to be a religious person. The only time he attended church was for weddings or funerals.

My father had been raised as an Anglican and attended church regularly. My mother was brought up in the United Church of Canada.

When one of my mother's sisters married a Catholic man, she had to convert to Catholicism. Dad, of course, went to the wedding with my mother.

Word reached the pastor of my father's church about his attending the nuptials. The pastor confronted my dad when he next saw him. "How dare you, a good Anglican, set foot inside a Catholic church?"

My father was livid. "You goddamn hypocrite," he replied. "My mother raised me to believe God doesn't care where you go to church as long as you go."

From that point on, my father never attended regular services.

A BAD INFLUENCE ON NORMALLY GOOD BOYS

My two oldest brothers, Harry and John, are less than two years apart. According to our father, they fought but it wasn't often and rarely found themselves in trouble.

A new family had moved in across the street. The mother was hoping the change in scenery would keep her son, Bobby, from shoplifting. She thought being around good families would be a positive influence on him.

One day, when my brothers were 10 or 11, Dad gave them enough money to go to the movies and nothing more. This day, Bobby tagged along with them.

When my father came home from work, Harry and Johnnie were outside, playing with toys he hadn't seen before. He asked Mum where the boys had gotten them from. She said she didn't know and he went out to ask them.

My brothers told him Bobby had shown them how to get things without having to pay for them. Dad was fuming – which didn't happen often – and told them they would have to return the items. They would also tell the owner what they had done.

It embarrassed them when Dad took them into the store to confront the owner. But, they admitted their wrongdoing and never did it again.

WHEN YOUR SON OFFERS A FAIR FIGHT

One of the foster children my parents took in was a blonde little cherub named Maureen. We had her for a few months until her mother found out we were looking after her. Her mother was a good friend of one of my cousins.

Her mother was living in the apartment building across the street with her new boyfriend. She complained to Social Services about us having her. The department decided Maureen would go back with her mother.

One night, two-year-old Maureen was being fussy as most are when they're tired. Her mother's boyfriend, who was drunk became frustrated with the child and beat her so bad she became deaf.

Social Services contacted my mother but she was in Brookfield, looking after my aunt's children while she was in hospital. She informed them she couldn't just up and leave 6 young children by themselves at the drop of a hat. It was late that night before we were home.

In the meantime, my brother, John, had found out what had

happened. As I mentioned in a previous story, Johnnie was a big man.

It took six guys to hold him back because he was going across the street to beat up the boyfriend. If he wanted a fight, John would make sure it was a fair one.

We ended up getting Maureen back for several months. They then gave her mother custody a second time. Several people saw her put the child in danger more than once afterwards.

This made my mother angry. She couldn't understand why Maureen would be given back after what had happened with the boyfriend.

Social Services took the child away for good from her mother. An elderly couple in Amherst eventually adopted her.

NEIGHBOURHOOD WATCH
GEORGE STYLE

Across the street from where we lived, there was a family who had a child with special needs. Donna would often "run away" from home. When she did, she was at our place or my uncle's next door.

When my brother, John, was about nine or ten, a new family moved into the area. A few days after they arrived, he saw the two boys throwing rocks at Donna and making fun of her.

John confronted them without a second thought. "I don't know what they do in England," he stated. "But, here in Canada, we don't throw rocks at people."

The boys stopped and never threw rocks again. In a twist of fate, one of the boys, Paul, became my brother's best friend and were inseparable until my brother passed away.

HOME PROTECTION

Quite a few years ago, when I was in my late twenties, I was working two full-time jobs. I would work midnight to 7:30 am at one job then 8:30 am to 4:30 pm at the other. It only gave me about five hours of sleep per night during the week.

One evening, a couple days after my aunt's place had been robbed; my mother went out to bingo and my dad visited a couple of friends. About an hour later, the phone rang. I didn't bother getting up to answer it as I knew it would take me more time to get back to sleep if I did.

Not long after that, I heard someone coming through the back door. I jumped out of bed, grabbed my Excalibur replica sword and met the "intruder." Good thing I stopped just before I swung. Turned out, it was my father.

"Why did you come in the back door?" I asked. He never came in the back.

"I thought it would be quieter," he responded. Considering my room was in the back, it didn't make much sense. He agreed after I explained that to him.

"But, if there is an intruder, don't stop," he stated.

MIKE THE BULLY

My youngest brother, Mike, was always smaller than other children until he was about 14 or 15. Even though he was two months premature, he still weighed six pounds six ounces.

One day, when Mike was about 8, there was a knock on the front door. A neighbor and his son faced Dad when he opened the door. The son was about 12 and twice the size of my brother.

The father told Dad about Mike beating up his son. Dad laughed. "My son beat him up?" he asked.

The man reiterated yes. Dad called for my brother, who came out of his bedroom. "So, again, you're telling me that my son here beat up your son?"

The other father turned red. He was angry and embarrassed. He grabbed his son, rushed him back across the street and giving him a lecture.

WHEN YOU'VE BEEN GIVEN A FAIR WARNING

When my mother was about 14, she worked at Conrad's Store where she had met my father.

One morning, an old drunk who lived nearby followed her. My Uncle Mike was watching from the living room window.

The drunk was saying something to Mum and giving her a hard time. She warned him to stop bothering her or else he'd get it.

Uncle Mike thought he should go out to see what he could do to help. By the time he reached the front steps, Mum had turned around and punched the man out.

My uncle wiped his hands together and thought, 'My work is done' and went back into the house. The neighbor next door, who witnessed the entire scene, laughed.

The man never smiled; let alone let out a laugh. He was nice and all; he didn't laugh. Even his wife had to get up from bed to see what was happening as she never heard him laugh either.

HAS YOUR POODLE HAD ALL ITS SHOTS?

My family and I used to drive to Ontario often to visit my Aunt Lizzie. She was one of Mum's sisters and had been battling cancer for quite some time.

On one particular visit, Mum and Dad drove through the United States instead of Quebec. My cousin, Patricia, and my brother, Tony, were with us on the trip.

At the border crossing, the Customs Officer asked if our poodle had all of its shots. It confused Mum and Dad since we didn't own a dog.

Tony was sleeping on Trisha's lap with a blanket over him. All you could see was the top of his curly head.

Trisha moved the blanket to reveal the sleeping toddler. Humiliated, the Customs Officer waved my father through. It never occurred to him to ask why a family of white people had a little brown baby.

FAMILY SECRETS

When my cousin, Trisha, was younger, she used to spend the night at my parents' place often. In the morning, she would have breakfast with my father.

Over the meal, she would tell him everything that had happened at her place throughout the week, including things her parents would not want made public.

When my cousin was older, she would often pester Dad to tell her what she told him but he would never tell her. To this day, she has no clue what family secrets she may have spilled.

GRANDDAD'S LITTLE MONKEY

Before Hanna was born and would spend the night with us, her sister, Brittany, would often come in to visit. Like Hanna, she would be with Dad more than Mum.

One day, she was in my room, watching television with my father and decided it would be a good idea to climb my bookshelves. When she reached the shelf that held my ceramic dog, she began to bark at it. Good thing she was over my bed in case she happened to fall.

If she wasn't pulling herself up on those shelves, she was making her way up the divider between the dining room and living room. Dad often scolded her, mainly because he was concerned she would fall and hurt herself. She would just turn around and laugh at him evilly.

TAKING A LEAP

When I was about four, my father was rebuilding the steps to the basement. I remember being at the top of where the stairs used to be and wanting to go down with Dad.

He kept telling me I had to stay where I was since there was no way for me to get down there. I didn't like this answer so I chose to jump. How I didn't get seriously hurt still has me scratching my head.

Dad took me to the hospital anyway, just to make sure there weren't any internal injuries. Luckily, I was fine but not so much another girl about my age.

When her mother heard why I was there, she tried to use the same excuse to explain her daughter's bumps and bruises. The medical staff stated they knew the difference between a fall (or in my case, a jump) and abuse.

DO YOU KNOW THAT MAN?

My brother, John, was always into sports – especially ones that were physical and rough. One sport he played was lacrosse.

He was playing a match at the Grey Arena and a player from the opposing team kept poking him with the end of his lacrosse stick.

Johnnie warned him to stop but, the guy continued to poke him. My brother had enough.

He grabbed the guy and knocked him down. John used his stick to hold him down while he tried to shake off his glove to punch him. He was determined to teach him a lesson.

A few years later, Johnnie was in visiting Mum when Dad came home. He was coming up the walk with one of the children's father. The man saw John sitting in the living room and asked Dad if he knew him.

Dad said, "Yes, that's my son."

He then asked my father if it was safe for him to go in. Dad asked him why. The man then went into the story about the lacrosse game. My father laughed but, told him it was okay to go inside.

NO BOYS ALLOWED

When Brittany was about five, her mother was pregnant with Hanna. Brittany was in one day to spend the night.

Dad and Brittany were in the backyard and talking with a neighbor. Jim knew Dad was about to have another grandchild.

He asked Brittany if she was going to have a brother or a sister. "No boys allowed in my house," she answered, annoyed by the question.

All Jim and Dad could do was laugh at her seriousness.

HALLOWEEN PRANK AT THE CRAIGS

As I wrote in a previous story, my grandfather Craig was quite the prankster. In the weeks leading up to Halloween one year, he heard a few teenagers talking about Mr. Craig and how they were not going to be fooled by him again this year.

He took a bar of lye soap, carved it into smalls squares and then covered them with chocolate. These special "candies" were for the teenagers only.

Most clued in to the prank but one young man actually took one and put it in his mouth. He realized too late but he was not about to give my grandfather the pleasure of knowing he fell for it.

My grandfather already knew and just chuckled under his breath.

ENLISTMENT

When my father was about fifteen, WWII was in its early stages. Two of Dad's brothers were already serving overseas.

My Dad wanted to do his part, so he left a note for his parents and headed for the enlistment office. He wasn't in line for long before my grandfather George showed up.

Granddad grabbed him and pulled him out of line. "I already have two sons over there; I don't need a third. Now, get yourself home."

AN EYE FOR AN EYE

Two of my mother's brothers served in the Second World War as well. My Uncle John was a paratrooper in northern Europe. My Uncle Harry – who everybody called Skipper – was stationed in northern Italy.

Uncle John was wounded in the chest and recuperating in a hospital in England in mid-December 1943. When he heard Skipper had been killed by a sniper in Italy, he got out of bed and began to get dressed. One of the nurses asked him what he was doing. "I'm going to kill the bastard who killed my brother," he responded.

It took the nurses several tries to put him back to bed. After the last time, the medical staff had to tie him down so he could recover from his own injury.

YOU'LL HAVE TO TALK PRETTY LOUD

When I lived in Iqaluit the first time, I would go to the post office a few times a week to check on mail and packages. One on such outing, I looked at the return address on one of the letters. I took a stutter step as I was surprised at what I saw.

The postmistress gave me a strange look. She had never seen me react like that to any of my mail.

The letter was from an ex-boyfriend I hadn't spoken to in several years. He had gotten married a couple years earlier and we had lost contact.

When I saw the return address, I initially thought it was from his parents telling me something had happened. But, then I recognized the handwriting and I wondered what he wanted.

He told me he had gotten a divorce and had subsequently moved back home. He said he was watching some late night show when a horoscope commercial came on and it featured Scorpio (my zodiac sign.)

The commercial reminded him of me. The next day, he called my parents' place and spoke with Dad.

My ex asked him if he could talk to me. "You'll have to talk pretty loud," my father answered.

When my ex asked why, Dad told him I was living up north. My ex thought that was pretty funny.

FRENCH IMMERSION

One summer, we were visiting my Aunt Fan in Cape Breton. I think I was about 13 or 14. Her son, David, and his family had come up to see us.

We were at the dinner table when David's wife, Cathy, mentioned Crystal was going into French Immersion when school started. Dad turned to Crystal and asked, "Why? Traci can teach you. She knows how to speak frog."

She turned to me and asked, "You can?"

I grinned and answered, "Yep. Ribbit. Ribbit."

BIRTHDAY PRANK

After my father left the dairy, he went to work at the Dartmouth Marine Slips. His first job was as a delivery man but the majority of his work was as a tug boat captain.

When the shipyard no longer needed the tug, they moved my father to work in the stores. The stores were where the supervisors would order supplies for use on the jobs.

One of Dad's co-workers at the store was Benny. Benny was about 6'2" or taller and close to 300 lbs. Despite his size, he was pretty easy-going and laid-back.

On Benny's birthday, Dad called him to the front of the store. When he came around the corner, Dad (who was standing on a chair) slapped a cream pie into the man's face.

Dad was ready to run, just in case. Luckily for him, Benny had a good sense of humor and took it as the joke it was.

TAKING DOWN UNCLE HARRY

Like my mother, Dad had a brother named Harry. My maternal Uncle Harry was about 5'5" and my paternal Uncle Harry was about 6'2". Although a big man, Harry was good-humored and could take a joke as well as he could give it.

He loved children but he and his wife were unable to have any of their own. When my oldest brother was about 3 (also named Harry just to add confusion), he was at my uncle's place waiting for him to come home.

When Uncle Harry came through the door, my brother came tearing around the corner and grabbed him by the legs. My uncle pretended to fall due to the grab from my brother.

My brother was ecstatic. "I got him! I got him!" he kept shouting.

PRESTON TAXI SERVICE

When Dad worked at the shipyard, one of his first jobs was as a delivery driver to different points in the city. He often delivered to Preston, which is a predominantly African-Canadian community. One on delivery, one of the men asked Dad if he could drop his wife off at the grocery store in town.

Dad said yes as he was heading there anyway. On his way back to Preston, he saw the same woman waiting for the bus with a load of groceries. He stopped and asked her if she wanted a lift back home and she gratefully accepted.

When he dropped her off, he refused to take any money she offered him. Because of his kindness, the elders in the community made certain no one gave him a hard time whenever he was out in the area.

HARRY'S WARNING

Back in the early 1940s, Dad, my paternal Uncle Harry and their brothers would often go to dances on Friday nights.

On one such night, Uncle Harry had a bit too much to drink and was not in the mood for joking around. He was sitting on the side of his car with his head in his hands.

One of his buddies decided it would be a good idea to jostle him about his current condition. Uncle Harry warned him to knock it off or else.

His friend decided to ignore the warning and kept at it and calling him names. My uncle finally had enough. He stood, his fist catching his friend's chin and knocking him to the ground.

Uncle Harry then resumed his position without saying a word.

WHEN YOUR KID GETS HERSELF SCARRED

When I was about 3, my mother was cleaning beneath the kitchen sink. Tony and I were playing nearby in the dining room.

She was nearly finished when the telephone rang. When she went to answer it, she left the front of the cupboard open.

I walked over to see if I could "help." I pulled out a nearly empty bottle of carpet cleaner and proceeded to shake it upside down. I was trying to get Mum's attention to let her know it was empty.

Some of the few remaining drops fell onto my polyester pants (it was the 1970s) and began burning through the material. I started to scream in pain as the chemicals seared into my upper thigh.

My father grabbed me, put me in a tub of cold water and tore off my pants. My parents took me to the hospital shortly after. The doctor told Dad if he hadn't thought on his feet, the scar on my leg would have been much worse than what it was – and is.

TWENTY QUESTIONS

When my brother, Mike, was about 3, our uncle, Jimmy, was building his house next door. Mike was fascinated by what he was doing. He began peppering our uncle with questions.

"Uncle Jimmy, what are you doing?"

"Mike, I'm busy."

"What's that for?"

"Mike, go home."

"Uncle Jimmy, what does that do?"

"Mike, your mother's calling you."

"Uncle Jimmy, why are you doing that?"

"Mike, just go home."

Obviously, my brother couldn't take a hint that he wasn't wanted. Either that or he just enjoyed annoying our uncle.

SULKY BABY

As mentioned previously, my father came from a large family. He was the seventh child of thirteen.

Many of his siblings – as well as Dad – had 3 or 4 children of their own so there were lots of cousins running around. One of my cousins, Dad's older sisters, Fanny.

They lived in Cape Breton. Aunt Fan was in Port Hawkesbury and Frances lived in Leitches' Creek.

We would often visit in summer (when we weren't visiting my Aunt Liz in Ontario). We would play cards most nights until about 1 in the morning.

My Uncle Doug was usually in bed before we started playing. Dad would regularly complain and whine about having to play cards to all hours in the morning.

On one visit – I was working so I couldn't go – my cousin, Frances, was down to visit. My father started on his complaining when it came time to play cards.

Frances wasn't hearing any of it. "Stop your whining, Sulky Baby, and have some fun," she ordered.

He complained a bit more so my cousin threatened to get him a soother to keep him from whining. The next time she saw him and he started his complaining, she handed him a gift.

When he opened it, he saw the blue soother. It was a present he kept until he passed away.

PAINTER'S APPRENTICE

When I was about two, Dad was afflicted with Bell's palsy. Bell's palsy is a paralysis or weakening of muscles on one side of the face.

Dad decided to take up painting as a hobby and to give him something to do while he was off work. He had everything set up downstairs to keep the paint fumes from stinking up the whole house.

I was in the basement with him one day. Instead of playing with toys, I decided to check out what Dad was doing with the paints.

I was making a mess and getting under Dad's foot. Every time he thought he had gotten rid of me, I found a way to go back to the basement.

I told him years later when he was showing a friend of mine some of his artwork and telling the story that I was only trying to help.

THE FOOTBALL STAR

When my brother, John, was in high school, he played football for the Dartmouth High School Spartans. He played both sides of the ball but he was more of a powerhouse on the defense.

My mother, although a tomboy, never understood the games of football or hockey. She did understand golf and baseball but not much else when it came to sports.

She decided to go watch a game with Dad. When my brother upended his opponent, my mother immediately stood up. "Johnnie, don't you hurt that boy!" she screamed.

The father sitting on the bench in front of her turned around. "That's the name of the game, lady," he replied.

Mum sat back down, a bit embarrassed. Fortunately, my brother couldn't hear what she had yelled but, chuckled when he was told of it afterwards.

DANCE PARTNERS

My cousin, Rhonda, was telling about how much she enjoyed watching my father and her mother dance. Dad and his sister, Joan, learned how to dance with each other.

The Georges, besides being known for talking, were also known for their great dancing ability. My mother and Aunt Helen (her sister who married my Dad's brother, Mickey) were also great dancers.

People loved seeing them work their magic on the dance floor. My nephew, Doug, mentioned getting lessons from his grandfather. Even one of the girls I worked with at Farrell Hall (who by chance was named Rhonda) asked my Dad to teach her how to dance.

At any event where dancing was involved, every family member would be involved. Those no related to us were in awe that we all got along and would dance with each other. It was, after all, who we were.

THE DOG FATHER

When I was around 9, my brother, Harry, brought a German shepherd puppy to the house. The dog was abandoned by a railroad near where he worked.

A commissionaire found him but he already had a houseful of pets so he gave him to Harry. The puppy didn't get along with Harry's cats or dog.

We ended up with the dog and he was named Casey by suggestion of my brother. Since he was found by a railroad, his full name was Casey Jones after the famous railroad engineer.

Casey spent most of time in the backyard, where he lorded over his kingdom. His kingdom was made up of the children my mother babysat and their friends.

It didn't matter if he never saw them before. If there was a child in his kingdom, he was their protector – aka their "Dog Father".

One father had offered to go out to get his sons but my mother said she should do it. Marty insisted he could get them.

By the time he stepped into the back porch, Casey had jumped onto the back steps, blocked the door with his body then turned and growled at him.

Marty jumped back as my niece, Tania, walked up, slapped Casey on the snout and told him to move out of the way. Marty said to Mum, "The size of me and the size of her; and I'm scared to death of him."

Another time, when my nephew, Doug was two or three, Casey was laying inside of his house. This was a rarity since he usually slept on the ground. My nephew had gone missing so Dad decided to look inside the dog house.

Doug was asleep inside, using Casey as a pillow. Dad reached in to take my nephew but Casey growled at him. Dad let him be and Doug came out on his own an hour or so later.

When Casey was still a pup, Harry and I were wrestling in the kitchen. I let out a scream and Casey came running in from the living room.

He grabbed my brother by the wrist and pulled him away from me. He never bit him but was making it known that my brother was not to hurt me.

NICKNAMES

When I put the word out I was looking for stories about my father, I started getting little anecdotes from friends and family. My niece, Tania, posted how Dad used to call her a little pest. Even when she visited him in the hospital, he said, "Glad to see you, pest."

Once she said that, Suzanne, one of the kids my mother looked after, said he would call her a pest as well. I think it was a nickname he gave most of the kids – especially to those he liked.

When I was smaller, he used to call my best friend at the time and I, Blackie and the Blonde Bombshell. Helen was Blackie and I was the Blonde Bombshell.

My niece, Hanna, used to call Dad, Granga, when she was 3 or 4. Dad seemed to rather enjoy being called that – probably because it was different.

FAST FOOD TRIPS

My nephew, Doug, who I mentioned before with the Dog Father story, had posted how I would take him to McDonald's whenever he wanted. This was true when we used to have a vehicle I was able to drive. If it wasn't to McDonald's, we went to Mr. Sub.

But, when Dad was the driver, we had to go to Harvey's. Dad and I preferred Harvey's over McDonald's but Doug didn't. He wasn't too fond of the fast food place when he was younger but he now wished there was a Harvey's close to him so he could have a burger in his grandfather's memory.

LADDER DROP

My cousin, Patricia, and her twin brother, Perry, were up at the house one weekend. My father was supposed to be watching them while he was fixing the roof.

My cousins were playing in a canoe in the backyard. Dad was on the roof with another person. One of them nudged the ladder and they couldn't grab it before it fell.

Fortunately, the ladder landed in between Perry and Patricia. I think my father was more upset than my cousins were. He knew if either of them had been injured, the guilt would have killed him.

SPECIAL REQUEST

When my parents were first going together, they and their friends would often take the ferry over to Halifax. They usually went over to take in a show.

While they were sitting on the top deck of the ferry, they would sing songs to entertain themselves. One day, the ferry boat captain came down to request a song. The gang was more than happy to oblige.

SCHOOL BOOKS

Another story my nephew posted was about the time his grandfather had donated books to his school. My father was a volunteer for the Independent Order of Foresters who often did work for the community.

One of the donations was a large selection of books to John MacNeil Elementary School in North End Dartmouth. The children were all required to write thank you notes to Dad. Doug's was the only one addressed to Granddad. I think Dad kept the letters until he passed away.

HOSPITAL VISIT

My father passed away on February 6, 2007 – exactly nine months before my birthday. I didn't visit my father in the hospital – I couldn't face seeing my father that way.

Doug had gone to visit him a couple of days before he died. Dad never had much energy but that day, he asked Doug to go for a walk with him. On this walk, Doug found out how much of a flirt my father was. It was also a walk he cherished.

LOCKED IN THE SHED

Two of the youngsters my mother looked after were Chris and Stephanie – brother and sister to Suzanne who I mentioned before. Stephanie posted about how she, Chris and Doug had gotten themselves locked inside our back shed.

Dad had to take the door off in order for them to get out. He was far from happy with them. Stephanie said they never saw him get angry so they knew they were in trouble. He told them he should make them re-hang the door as punishment for their crime.

SMACK ON THE BEHIND

Tania's daughter, Brittany – the subject of some of my previous stories – was spending a couple of days in town with Nanny and Granddad. Dad and Brittany decided to take a walk up to the beach.

Brittany thought it would be a good idea to run off. When Dad caught up to her, he gave her a quick crack on her butt.

Tania said he told her about it but she said he had her permission to do it again if Brittany ever pulled it again. She felt Dad felt guilty when he did it because he wasn't the type to hurt a fly.

SCOTLAND TRIP

For years, I heard from Dad how much he wanted to visit Scotland; the country where his mother was born and raised. I told him shortly before he retired, he now had the opportunity to go. He said it was too late – he was too old and any close relatives would now be deceased.

Five years after he passed away, I made the decision to go to Scotland. This trip was going to be for Dad since he never made it while he was alive.

I was on the shuttle bus to the Halifax Airport and sitting pretty much alone. There was no one sitting in the row in front or in back of me.

I heard a voice whisper in my ear to look outside. I glanced to my right, confused. The voice repeated itself, this time with annoyance.

When I looked out the window, my eyes veered towards the sky. Between two dark grey clouds was the form of an angel.

At the time, I thought it was my brother who had recently passed. But, after I came home and thought about it,

I believed it had to be my father, letting me know he was coming with me.

Dad always told me my grandmother was from Barrhead. I found out later she was actually from Carluke. Since this trip was only for three full days, I didn't think I would be able to make it to Barrhead.

On my second full day, I had booked myself the Hop-On Hop-Off Bus Tour of Glasgow. The last stop I decided to jump off at was at Central Station.

I went into one of the shops called The Heritage of Scotland. Since I had missed Mother's Day, I thought I would buy something for my mother while I was there. I went in specifically to find items with her maiden name of Craig.

I ended up purchasing more than I had planned. The store owner advised me that I could claim the VAT since I was a visitor. She gave me the directions of where I should go but somehow ended up somewhere else.

I found myself in the train station. I decided to check out the kiosks to see where trains at this particular station traveled.

When I saw the village of Barrhead, I made the snap decision to purchase a ticket. I figured even if I didn't spend a lot of time there, at least I could say I went.

After taking some photos, I made my way back to catch the train to Glasgow. I noticed a young woman walking up the street and I had to do a double take.

Except for the hair color, she was identical to my cousin, Vicki. She even had the same gait as Vicki. I fought the urge to run up to her and ask if she was related to the Cullen family.

I had a great time visiting the country of my ancestors. I just hope my father did as well.

CPSIA information can be obtained
at www.ICGtesting.com
Printed in the USA
BVHW031359290722
643329BV00015B/1081